Nietzsche and Postmodernism

Dave Robinson

ICON BOOKS UK

TOTEM BOOKS USA

Published in the UK in 1999
by Icon Books Ltd., Grange Road,
Duxford, Cambridge CB2 4QF
email: icon@mistral.co.uk
www.iconbooks.co.uk

Published in the USA in 1999
by Totem Books
Inquiries to: PO Box 223,
Canal Street Station,
New York, NY 10013

Distributed in the UK, Europe,
Canada, South Africa and Asia
by the Penguin Group:
Penguin Books Ltd.,
27 Wrights Lane,
London W8 5TZ

In the United States,
distributed to the trade by
National Book Network Inc.,
4720 Boston Way, Lanham,
Maryland 20706

Published in Australia in 1999
by Allen & Unwin Pty. Ltd.,
PO Box 8500, 9 Atchison Street,
St. Leonards, NSW 2065

Library of Congress Catalog
Card Number: 99-071122

ISBN 1 84046 093 8

Typesetting by Wayzgoose

Printed and bound in the UK by
Cox & Wyman Ltd., Reading

Nietzsche the Prophet

Nietzsche is an important philosopher because he was the first to recognise what being 'modern' really means for Western Europeans. He saw that two thousand years of belief in Christian values was coming to an end, and that this meant that our individual lives no longer had any purpose or meaning. Even worse, nearly all of the key ideas and values of Western thought were just 'metaphysics', without foundation, and he believed that this devastating fact would have to be confronted honestly. He finally suggested the need for 'new people' who would understand and celebrate this new state of affairs. And all of these disturbing ideas he expressed in an extraordinary way:

At last the horizon appears free again to us, even granted that it's not bright, at last our ships may venture out again. . . . the sea, our sea lies open again; perhaps there never has been such an 'open sea'.[1]

Nietzsche knew he was a prophet. Photographs of him usually reveal a man with a ridiculous walrus moustache and wild staring eyes. He always thought he was writing for a more appreciative future audience, and described himself as a 'posthumous' philosopher. So, one hundred years later, perhaps we are that audience and he is the first great postmodernist . . .

A Warning

But Nietzsche spoke in many different voices. His philosophy is contradictory, figurative and ironic. Since his death, his words have been deconstructed and reconstructed in all sorts of ways. There have been poets and playwrights, anarchists, fascists, existentialists and postmodernists who have all described themselves as 'Nietzschean'. So there seems to be a different Nietzsche for every age.

Nietzsche: the Life in Brief

Nietzsche was born in 1844 in Röcken, Germany, the son of an austere Lutheran Pastor. He was a bit of an adolescent prodigy – a talented linguist and a gifted amateur musician. As a student, he lost his Christian faith quite early on, and gave up his theological studies to become a brilliant young classicist. At the age of 24, he was appointed professor of classical philology at the University of Basel.

His life changed dramatically when he got hold of a copy of Schopenhauer's *The World as Will and Idea* (1818). It was a book that confirmed his own atheism and enabled him to systematise his thoughts into some sort of coherent world view. As a young man, he was introduced to Wagner and his wife, Cosima, and was bewitched by both of them during his early years. His first major book, *The Birth of Tragedy* (1872), is dedicated to Wagner. He subsequently wrote a series of aphoristic books that criticise Western civilisation, such as *Human, All Too Human* (1878). In the late 1870s, Nietzsche's general health went into a gradual decline and he finally had to resign his professorship.

Nietzsche was unwell for most of his adult life, and may have had syphilis. He suffered from a variety of ailments, including headaches, insomnia and near blindness which sometimes drove him close to suicidal despair. He spent much of the rest of his life in futile wanderings around Europe trying to recover his health. It's pretty obvious that his own personal struggles against illness inform his philosophical message. Nietzsche thought modern civilisation was diseased, infected by the toxins of Christianity and nihilism, and his mission was to provide a remedy.

By 1882, he was writing *Thus Spake Zarathustra*, in which he put forward the two ideas for which he is most famous: the 'Overman' and 'Eternal

Return'.* In the last years of his life he became increasingly isolated and ill, but amazingly prolific, with books like *Beyond Good and Evil* (1885), *The Genealogy of Morals* (1887), *The Anti-Christ* (1888) and *The Will to Power* (published post-humously in 1910). They're odd books, full of strange poetic aphorisms and ironic assertions, expressed in a language that seems neither literal nor figurative, but somewhere puzzlingly in between. Partly because of these stylistic excesses, his philosophy was largely ignored by most of his contemporaries, and his later work is often bitter and dogmatic as a result. However, he always remained confident that his day would come.

I want to be right not for today or tomorrow but for the millennia . . . [2]

By 1888, his behaviour had become increasingly bizarre, and he was finally diagnosed as insane. He spent the last years of his life being cared for by his sister Elizabeth – an unpleasant woman who later edited her brother's works into crude anti-Semitic propaganda. He died in Weimar in 1900.

*There is a section at the back of this book explaining the key ideas relating to Nietzsche's work.

Nietzsche and the Collapse of Christianity

Nietzsche thought that Western Europeans should face up to the fact that Christian values were no longer credible. Anyone who continued to believe in them was dishonest or 'inauthentic'. The various 'faiths' replacing Christianity were equally bankrupt, especially the worship of science and progress. When the mass of people finally saw the emptiness of these newer values, a terrible form of pessimistic nihilism would result. Civilisation would be left with nothing to believe in, and would collapse. As a previously very devout Lutheran who became a militant atheist, perhaps Nietzsche overemphasised the dangers of a secular society.

The Greeks

He would have denied it, but Nietzsche was a Utopianist, and a reactionary. He believed there was one 'Golden Age' against which all other historical periods, including his own, could be measured. He had a vision, and, unsurprisingly for a classical scholar, he found it in Ancient Greece:

The Greeks are interesting and quite disproportionately important because they had such a host of

7

great individuals . . . These men are integral, entire and self-contained, and hewn out of stone . . . They are not bound by convention.[3]

The 'Greeks' referred to here are early 6th century BC thinkers like Thales, Heraclitus and Empedocles, not the later Athenian philosophers like Socrates, Plato and Aristotle. He admired these 'pre-Socratics' because he thought they were noble, free, creative and passionate. The later Athenians were inferior because they believed in different things: an absolute morality, the immortality of the soul, transcendent realities, and the power of human reason. Athenian philosophy also helped soften up Western civilisation for the eventual arrival of Christianity – an even bigger disaster.

Nietzsche's view was that modern man over-valued his 'Apollonian' nature at the expense of his 'Dionysian' qualities. Both are necessary aspects of the human psyche, but the Apollonian disciplined intellect is usually overvalued. Being 'Dionysian' for Nietzsche meant being strong and courageous, accepting the harshness and arbitrary suffering that life as it is can dole out, and yet still saying a final, cheerful, exuberantly mad-and-merry 'Yes' to life. The pre-Socratic Greeks had no faith in phoney transcendent values. Instead, they faced up to and coped with the brutal realities of human existence extremely well. So modern men should be able to learn from their example.

Nietzsche's analysis of classical Greek culture is deeply personal, poorly substantiated, and often fantastic. But he fervently *believed* it. He spent the rest of his life producing his own odd mixture of philosophy, psychology and myth, advancing this kind of passionate stoicism as a cure for Western ills.

Against Christianity and Transcendence

What was really wrong with Western civilisation was Christianity – a religion for which Nietzsche seems to have had a passionate Oedipal hatred. (He was the son of three generations of strict Lutheran preachers.) His later philosophy is full of outbursts like this:

I call Christianity the one great curse, the one enormous and innermost perversion, the one great instinct of revenge for which no means are too venomous, too underhand, too underground and too petty – I call it the one immortal blemish of mankind.[4]

Nietzsche's view was that Christianity was the latest and most pernicious stage in a peculiar way of thinking that began with Socrates. Socrates encouraged the belief in immortal souls and absolute truths. His disciple Plato devised a 'two-world' philosophy, which claimed that this everyday material world is an inferior copy of a perfect transcendent one. These beliefs in 'higher' (or 'transcendent') truths and existences blended easily into the subsequent theology of the Christian Church. Christian values and beliefs then inevitably influenced modern Western philosophy, notably that of 'the Enlightenment'. Descartes, the first 'modern' philosopher, 'proved' the existence of immortal souls, as well as certain eternal truths of mathematics and science. The German philosopher Kant pronounced the existence of another superior 'noumenal' world that our human senses can never reach. Western philosophers have fooled themselves into believing in the possibility of absolute and total kinds of knowledge. They have brought forth escapist fantasies about transcendent worlds. It was a philosophical tradition that Nietzsche was determined to finish off.

Schopenhauer and the Will to Power

Arthur Schopenhauer (1788–1860) also insisted that these kinds of transcendent philosophy were nonsense. There is only one certain truth that lies 'behind' our phenomenal world and that is the existence of a constant energetic struggle or 'Will' which only a few determined individuals can ever choose to avoid. Nietzsche agreed, but thought that the 'Will' that determined everything was 'the Will to Power'. All beings exist in a state of continuous strife, but the conflict is creative, healthy and productive.

This world: a monster of energy, without beginning, without end; an immovable, brazen enormity of energy, which does not grow bigger or smaller; which does not expend itself but only transforms itself. . . . And any other philosophical views are basically superfluous pernicious nonsense.[5]

Like Schopenhauer, Nietzsche was a profound sceptic. Everything is open to suspicion because human beings continually delude themselves into believing that they have knowledge when they don't. Philosophical scepticism usually comes in different forms. Most philosophers tend to be *selective* sceptics as a matter of course. They often declare that all previous philosophies are invalid, but that their own truths are cast-iron. Some, like Nietzsche, are more worryingly *global*. They contend that there is no such thing as human knowledge, and that 'truth' is either unreachable or worse, a myth.

Anti-Foundationalism

Nietzsche's brand of global scepticism is usually called 'anti-foundational', a term that needs a bit of explanation. As King Lear famously says, quoting Aristotle, 'Nothing will come of nothing'. All philosophy has to start with some core beliefs that are thought to be 'self-evident' and therefore true. This is where 'metaphysics' creeps in, something that Nietzsche was rather good at detecting. There are, for example, some things you just have to accept if scientific accounts of the world are to work, like the actual existence of a physical world separate from our perception of it, and that our perception of it is roughly accurate, and that causation works in one direction only. These are all sensible beliefs, but hard to prove. It just isn't possible to 'climb out' of our own sensory experience of the world to check that there is a world out there conveniently providing reliable sensory experiences for us. And, although we haven't experienced an effect that preceded a cause yet, that's no guarantee that such an event isn't possible. Nietzsche insisted that our modern Western belief systems were founded on a whole series of metaphysical assumptions like these.

The Enlightenment

Modern European civilisation is 'Christian'. It's also a product of 'the Enlightenment', a cultural phenomenon that began somewhere towards the end of the 17th century. There is always much debate about what the Enlightenment was, and whether we are still living in it. It is part of our cultural and historical tradition, and massively influential on Western science and political life.

Enlightenment philosophers like Descartes claimed that it was our reason that made us 'human'. So long as we restrict ourselves to certain kinds of philosophical and scientific inquiry, he claimed, we can use our intellect to obtain infallible knowledge. Reason is universal, objective and autonomous, and when used according to a 'method', enables science and society to progress.

Rousseau had less faith in reason and science than Descartes, but still believed in political progress. If you appeal to the rational autonomy of individuals and can persuade them to agree to replace their 'natural' liberty with 'civil' liberty, then human beings can create a virtually perfect political society.

Other Enlightenment thinkers like Kant used this faith in rational thought and autonomy to reinforce Christian ethical beliefs. Practical reason could produce universal and absolute moral laws that were eternally true and so compulsory for everyone.

It was Enlightenment ideas like these that gave Europeans confidence in the certainty of future scientific, moral and political progress. Their influence continued into the 19th century and remained unquestioned until Nietzsche examined them more closely.

Nietzsche had a startlingly cosmic perspective on this naive Enlightenment faith in human reason and progress:

In some remote corner . . . of the universe there was once a star on which clever animals invented knowledge. It was the most arrogant and mendacious moment of 'universal history' . . . [6]

Nietzsche refused to accept the 'correspondence theory' of truth. This maintains that our mental concepts somehow 'tally' with the world because we always have direct access to 'reality' either through our senses or our reason. For Nietzsche, the only *real* truth about us and the world is the irrepressible 'Will to Power' of everything and its energetic need to control. This means that human beings only ever create 'truths' for themselves that are useful and help them to survive as a species. 'Knowledge' and 'Truth' are only effective instruments, not transcendent entities. They are concepts that human beings invent. But they can never be 'objective' because they always serve some human interest or purpose.

Nietzsche never developed a consistent or very coherent 'theory of knowledge', and he often expressed his views in playful metaphorical aphorisms. But in essence he agreed with Heraclitus that the 'becoming' universe is always in a state of continual chaotic movement and change, so that any stability or coherence we find is that which we ourselves have invented. 'To know' means something like 'to impose categories upon chaotic processes that make the world useful to us and give us a sense of power and control'. Even mathematics and logical deduction are merely human contrivances, 'presuppositions with which nothing in the real world corresponds'.[7]

Words, Reality and Thoughts

One key essay, which certainly sounds very post-modern, is 'On Truth and Falsity in their Extra-Moral Sense', first published in 1873. Here Nietzsche suggests that all language is inevitably 'metaphorical'. The essay begins with yet another critical account of the contrasting differences between Dionysian creativity and Apollonian intellect. The human intellect must always be fundamentally deceitful because individuals have to live together. Social and intellectual life depends on common consent, and this gives birth to a shared consensual reality in which such concepts as 'knowledge' inevitably emerge. These concepts are then reinforced by language. Such limited human 'truths' are harmless enough, because they make social life possible. Unfortunately, they can also lead to a futile hunt for spurious and illusory metaphysical 'truths' that just don't exist. Either way, human language has no coherent correspondence with the 'real' world. Language can never be 'literal' in the sense that it can describe the reality of the world to us. Concepts like 'truth' and 'knowledge' are relative to language, or 'metaphorical', and can only ever lie within language – they can tell us nothing about the world. Nietzsche's radical view of the relationship between language and the world pre-echoes many of the central ideas of 20th century philosophers like Wittgenstein and Derrida.

Nietzsche also saw language as the key player in a continual process of human self-deception. Words are what we think with, and we often automatically assume that there are entities 'out there' to which they refer. Words are useful to us because we can use them to simplify and 'freeze' the chaos and complexities of our surroundings, but that is all they can do. Not only will our grammar control the ways in which our thoughts are organised, but more drastically, it will determine what sorts of thoughts it is possible for us to have. So the subject-predicate grammar we think with means that we impose a subject-object framework onto the world, and this encourages us to believe, for example, that there is an 'ego' or an 'I' that exists as a transcendent Cartesian entity somehow inside us, separate from our physical existence.

The Problem of Logic

The Enlightenment and all of its interlocking theories on knowledge, ethics and politics is, at bottom, founded on an unshakeable belief in reason. For most 18th century philosophers, 'reason' meant the same as 'reasoning' or logic. Deductive logic is at the very heart of all Enlightenment thought. But if logic cannot be guaranteed as a method of discovering new knowledge or clarifying concepts, then the whole Enlightenment project is in trouble. Nietzsche's view is that it is impossible for human beings to have objective thoughts – people are always driven by passions and desires, often in ways of which they are unaware. Logic is only a reflection of how our minds work, and has nothing to do with objective knowledge or truth.

The Athenian philosopher Aristotle was clever enough to realise that you have to obey a few 'laws' if logic is to work. One law of logic is the 'Law of Contradiction', which states that nothing can be simultaneously *both* A and not-A. (Nothing can be both a giraffe and not a giraffe at the same time.) Nietzsche's view is that this 'rule' is merely 'a course of logical thinking and concluding in our present brain [which] corresponds to a process and struggle of drives which in themselves individually are all very illogical'.[8] So logic does not reflect the world or offer any kind of truth guarantees. It is just our human way of creating a convenient 'reality' that we find adequate to our needs.

It gets worse. There are all kinds of metaphysical

assumptions underlying logic, like the belief that everything can be generalised and put into homogenous groups (giraffes). Even 'things' themselves (the giraffe) are just 'constructs' that we invent for our convenience and sanity. Logic, in other words, is merely a method of rearranging fictional constructs that very likely have no correspondence in reality, and it depends on metaphysical assumptions that may well be false.

Logic and classification both originate from our need to control and dominate the world.

But this prevailing tendency to treat the similar at once as identical, is an illogical tendency – for nothing is identical – which first created all the foundations of logic.[9]

The undoubted usefulness of logic hypnotises human beings into believing that they can use it to obtain transcendent or scientific truths. Logic is a very useful survival tool, but that is *all* it is.

The Demolition of Science

If reason and logic are suspect, then there isn't much hope for scientific 'truth' either. Nietzsche insists that science can never provide us with objective truths because they don't exist.

It is sufficient to regard science only as the most fruitful possible humanization of things; we learn to describe ourselves more and more exactly by describing things and the succession of things.[10]

Nietzsche's critical analysis of scientific laws owes a lot to the work of the 18th century Scottish radical empiricist and sceptic David Hume. Hume was always very doubtful about the grandiose claims made by many European Rationalist philosophers. Most scientific laws are based on observed regularities in nature. It's very easy for philosophers and scientists then to convince themselves that these regularities are eternal and compulsory, or even divinely ordered. But there is no convincing proof that any of this is so.

Nietzsche attacked the very idea that the natural world is rationally ordered and obedient to a set of discoverable natural laws. Any investigation into science as a historical, cultural and social phenomenon soon shows that scientific 'truths' are always changing. Scientific 'laws' are contingent human constructs. They are often thought to be rather more than that – but only because of the persuasiveness of words like 'law'.

Nature's conformity to 'law' of which you physicists talk so proudly . . . exists only owing to your interpretation and bad philology. . . . Things do not behave regularly, according to a rule: there are no things . . . they behave just as little under the constraint of a necessity . . . and our entire science still lies under the misleading influence of language . . .[11]

Perspectivism, Progress and Nihilism

Another of Nietzsche's sceptical arguments is based on historical relativism. If history shows us that there have been widely different accounts of how the universe is constructed, what guarantee do we have that our current model is the correct one? Nietzsche's doctrine of 'perspectivism' claims that there can only ever be imperfect interpretations and never absolute truths about the world. This view of science as a cultural, limited and very human activity, is one that has influenced many 20th-century philosophers of science such as Thomas Kuhn and Paul Feyerabend.

Science is the final malign offspring of the Enlightenment, and so merely one temporary interpretation of the world. But Nietzsche saw that most modern Europeans didn't recognise this fact. Their faith in science and scientific progress was a dangerous illusion. Scientific progress will not always produce human happiness:

It is perhaps just dawning on five or six minds that physics too is only an interpretation and exegesis of the world (to suit us, if I may say so!) and not a world explanation.[12]

Nietzsche's remedy was to recommend a new pragmatic 'joyful science' aware of its own bias and limitations. It is quite possible for us to observe the world and use these observations to enable civilisation to progress. But what we should never believe is that science can somehow discover absolute truths. Modern 'scientism' – the blind worship of science – is only a shallow substitute for religion. Religion and science both made grandiose claims that Nietzsche thought could never be justified. The collapse of both belief systems would soon lead to universal nihilism, despair, and the collapse of the civilised world.

Belief in the Self

Cartesian philosophical certainties are, to a large extent, what gave the Enlightenment its confidence. European philosophy relied on the guaranteed authenticity of the existence of the self – the 'Cogito' – the one thing that Descartes claimed to be indubitable. *Cogito ergo sum.* I think therefore I am.

But Nietzsche's critical analysis of the 'self' concluded that it is as much a myth as any scientific 'law'. We cling to a belief in a central core of identity because we need it. It helps us to have a consistent grip on our experiences. It is a convenient fiction that is necessary for the preservation of our form of life. But because we believe in it and need it, that in no sense guarantees the truth of its existence.

There is thinking; consequently there is that which thinks – that is [all that] Descartes' argument comes to . . . merely a formulation of our grammatical habit, which posits a doer for what is done.[13]

Linguistic determinism is again the cause of our belief in the self. Western languages depict the world in subject-predicate terms, so we see everything always in terms of performers and performances. Nietzsche's view is that there is no substance or cause corresponding to that which we call the ego or the 'I'. Linguistic camouflage hides the truth from us, which is that reality is made up of processes and change. Human beings cannot exist somehow independently of these huge, fundamental forces of nature and history that Nietzsche calls the 'Will to Power'. We fool ourselves when we believe that we are uniquely individual or that our will power is exclusively our own. This means that political and moral philosophies (like those of Rousseau and Kant) are misguided because they rely on a naive belief in personal autonomy as a first premise.

The Genealogy of Morals

This demolition of the self and of free-will brings us to Nietzsche's *moral* scepticism. Nietzsche was determined that modern Europeans would have to re-evaluate the origins of all their ethical beliefs. In the 1870s, he published an essay called 'The Use and Abuse of History', a study of what history is, how it comes to be written, and what it is ultimately used for. Nietzsche then carried out an aggressive investigation of the past in order to reveal the true 'genealogies' of modern moral values. History determines who we are and the values we believe in, usually in ways of which we are utterly unaware. Human beings like to think of themselves as autonomous, ahistorical beings, but they are always the products of a complex social and political past.

Nietzsche's eventual conclusion was that we have been made weak and passive by a Christian morality that makes free-will, responsibility, 'guilt' and 'sin' all prerequisites of 'goodness'. For Greek philosophers, the word 'good' had *factual* content, and applied to people rather than actions. A 'good man' was a good specimen of Athenian humanity, not just someone who blindly obeyed an ethical doctrine. Nietzsche's romantic views about the pre-Socratic Greeks meant that, for him, they became something close to ideal human beings. Pre-Christian Greeks were powerful individuals of instinct and passion, spontaneous and creative, men who actualised themselves in ways that the 'herd morality' of Christianity forbids.

Nietzsche's genealogical researches into Western moral beliefs reveal several key stages in their development. Moral codes are initially imposed and externally reinforced with harsh punishment and discipline. Each individual's constant fear of reprisal is a great inducement to memory training, and this then leads to the acceptance of a personal sense of responsibility. The whole process finally produces 'sovereign' individuals let loose on moral auto-pilot who have internalised society's moral rules into their 'conscience'. They become components of a society whose morality is designed to make human beings 'regular, calculable and uniform'. Nietzsche's explanation of morality is therefore ruthlessly 'naturalist' (psychological, anthropological and sociological). There are no references to 'reason' or transcendent and metaphysical entities in his account.

Christian Values and Nihilism

Modern morality is still essentially Christian. But Christianity originated amongst subject peoples, many of whom were slaves. Christian values inevitably reflect these social and political circumstances. For Nietzsche, all human values are always a reflection of some power struggle, the result of one group wishing to impose its own values onto others. Christian or 'slave' values are born out of resentment and repression, and so are the result of projected hostility. Slaves are able to sublimate their feelings of impotent rage by inventing a new kind of ethics, a code of behaviour that emphasises humility, conscience, asceticism, free-will and blame. Christianity is a 'herd morality' that attracts and produces people who are pessimistic and timid. It is also a pernicious value system because it stands in the way of evolution and the eventual production of new and superior kind of human being.

For Nietzsche, there is nothing 'natural' or mystical about Christian (or any) morality. It is an ideology like any other, and based on denial. It encourages a belief in the repression of instinct, and thwarts creative energies. As a moral code it produces dull, static and conformist societies that dampen down human potential and achievement. What is true of Christian ethics is equally true of political philosophies that rely on myths like those of the 'autonomous' individual and social contracts. Societies built on such doctrines merely answer the needs of the weak and insecure.

Nietzsche was convinced that Christianity would eventually self-destruct because it advocates the search for eternal, transcendent 'truths', and this inevitably leads to science and the fatal investigation of its own metaphysics. A naive worship of science itself may then briefly become a secular substitute for Christianity. But science is only one limited human method of investigating natural phenomena. It cannot create a coherent set of values. The recognition of its limitations will in turn produce deep feelings of disillusionment and pessimistic nihilism. And that's the situation that the modern world finds itself in today.

Assessing Nietzsche's Scepticism

Nietzsche's scepticism is certainly radical, although it's not always clear how coherent or 'global' it actually is. His philosophy makes all kinds of pronouncements, some of which are ironic, some of which are purposely designed to shock. So, for example, Nietzsche seems hostile to the elevation of scientific knowledge as a panacea for all human problems, yet at other times is full of admiration for its achievements. It all depends on which bits you read.

Global scepticism always produces paradoxes and empty circularities. How can Nietzsche's own subversive claims to know the limitations of human knowledge survive his own scepticism? If there is no 'truth' or 'knowledge', how can we accept Nietzsche's epistemological claim that all of reality can be reduced to 'energy' or Will to Power? If 'perspectivism' means that all truths are merely interpretations that serve differently successful forms of life, then the actual claim that this is the case, is itself merely the victorious result of such a struggle. Nietzsche does occasionally admit that his own philosophy is just one interpretation, because that is all it can be. But if this is the case, then why should we take any of his philosophy that seriously? It also seems incoherently self-defeating to use language to claim that language is itself relentlessly metaphorical. Criticisms like these have also been made against some postmodernist philosophy. In the end, perhaps all we can do is to produce deconstructive re-readings of Nietzsche's texts and celebrate all the paradoxes they produce.

Nietzsche is undoubtedly a shrewd investigator of the shaky genealogical foundations of most modern Western beliefs and values. But are his more positive philosophical ideas as profound and unique as he thought they were? Nietzsche rejected all philosophy – and then produced another that looks remarkably metaphysical. His radical scepticism stems from the 'fact' that there is but one truth – the 'Will to Power' – which means that all other philosophical or scientific explanations of anything become invalid and illusory. But it's never very clear exactly what the 'Will to Power' actually *is*. If the whole of creation operates according to this relentless force, what sort of power is it? What sort of energy is being referred to? Is the 'Will to Power' a scientific, cosmological and biological fact? Is it a psychological analysis? Or is it yet another metaphysical foundation put in place to justify those unique values that Nietzsche just happens to admire?

The *Übermensch* and Eternal Return

In his most famous work, *Thus Spake Zarathustra* (1884), Nietzsche finally clarified those two doctrines for which he is most famous: the 'Overman' and the myth of 'Eternal Return'. These are his remedies against the chaos and nihilistic despair that he suggests will eventually envelop the Western world after the collapse of Christian and scientific world views.

The *Übermensch* – translated either as Overman or Superman – is a new kind of being, a superior character who will be able to leave behind the pull of human gravity. Overmen will be powerful, strong and healthy individuals, who live an earthly and sensuous life, free from the error of belief in some transcendent reality and the restrictions of 'herd morality'. They will readily accept the absurdity of the human condition and will become artistic creators of themselves and a new pan-European society. Their robust culture will concentrate on artistic rather than metaphysical works. Rather more routine and mundane work will be performed by a slave caste. But Overmen will not be cruel fascist bullies. Once they have conquered and recreated themselves, gone 'beyond' human nature, then they will be tolerant and decent to the lower orders they rule over.

Nietzsche's future society is splendidly vague on detail. It's a reactionary fantasy based on his own worship of pre-Socratic Greek culture. Nowhere does Nietzsche explain or discuss the legitimacy of his bizarre authoritarian political system. He offers no suggestions as to what kind of civil law would apply when the passionate and instinctive intensity of his Overpeople's lives led to disputes.

However, this idea of the Overman as a special kind of individual did have an immense influence on Existentialist philosophers like Martin Heidegger (1889–1976) and Jean-Paul Sartre (1905–80). If there is no God and there are no eternal verities, and the universe in which we live is 'absurd', then Nietzsche has a point. We do have to *create* ourselves. Who we *are* is decided by the choices we make and the acts we perform. And the process of creating ourselves may well be rather like that of the artist. But this is not a book about Existentialism.

Eternal Return

If there is no God, then there is probably no personal or eternal afterlife either. Nietzsche's perspective on time seems to have been unusually huge. He was continually aware of the presence of the distant past, and he wrote for the future. The doctrine of the Eternal Return is his own version of eternity. It envisages history working in vast repetitive cycles, so that the 'meaning' of life is found within life itself. Nietzsche typically presents his idea sometimes as a literal scientific truth about the cosmos, and sometimes as a kind of moral and psychological metaphor. Once we know that our choices and actions are endlessly repeated, then presumably we will be very careful as to what they are. We will be more concerned with the future than dominated by the past, which means only *we* can ever have the responsibility for *who* we eventually become.

But Nietzsche's account of Overmen and their Eternal 'Returns' seems full of paradoxes. If time repeats itself, then how can the *Übermensch* go in for any kind of process of 'becoming'? The French philosopher Gilles Deleuze famously suggested that the myth is a Nietzschean version of Kant's Categorical Imperative ('Never perform an action you would not be willing to see endlessly repeated'). But even if this is a correct interpretation, then the individual moral lives of Overmen could only be much less spontaneous.

In spite of all these internal inconsistencies and paradoxes, Nietzsche remains a great philosopher.

He is in the first division – but not because he provides us with devastatingly convincing *answers* to the human condition and convincing blueprints for its future development. He is important because he asks original *questions* that had never really been asked before with such intensity. The questions may be more psychological and sociological than philosophical, but they remain very 'modern' ones:

Why do human beings have this craving for eternal transcendent truths that cannot possibly exist, and why are they so ready to deceive themselves with fantasies?

Can human beings and their societies survive on shabby outmoded ideals and values that no-one really believes in any more?

If we are going to choose to be teleological about ourselves, what sort of ideals, goals and purposes are we going to give ourselves, and for what reasons?

Nietzsche was the first philosopher to ask questions about the unique nature of modern life and its accompanying sense of doubt and loss. He invented a new kind of 'genealogical' history in order to investigate how we have got where we are, and makes some suggestions as to what we should do about it. He has a bold, if rather incoherent, set of projects that he thinks might be solutions to our problems of being 'all too human'. He is a great believer in the role that art can play in making human life understandable and bearable, so that we can at least recognise and even celebrate where we are, after many centuries of self-deception.

Postmodernism and Nietzsche

Nietzsche thought that all the 'grand narratives' of his day were in a state of collapse. Enlightenment faith in reason and progress would inevitably produce political systems that suppressed originality and human potential. Science could never be a source of values by which human beings were able to live. Beliefs in reason and logic, science and its 'laws', 'truth' and 'knowledge', are all without foundation. Nietzsche even disputed the existence of a conscious subject who could think in a language with stable meanings. The only reliable truth is the 'Will to Power' – which is relentless and eternal.

All of these ideas seem very 'postmodernist', so it's no surprise that Nietzsche has often been adopted as the great-grandfather of our own more recent postmodern beliefs. Indeed, many postmodernist philosophers, like Derrida and Foucault, have written essays that forcefully make this claim. Creative re-readings of Nietzsche gave many late

20th-century French intellectuals the confidence to get out from under the dominant Marxist paradigm, in order to see the modern world in different ways and to create new kinds of philosophy. Many postmodernist philosophers also felt that they were presiding over the final disintegration of the European Enlightenment project, so confidently predicted by Nietzsche. Unlike him, though, they don't seem to have such a clear programme for the future of civilisation.

But what is Postmodernism?

Nobody really knows what the label 'postmodernism' means. At least two famous 'postmodernist' philosophers have now disowned the term as vacuous, ambiguous and misleading. No-one is even sure what 'modernism' means, let alone in what sense we have recently gone 'beyond' it, or rejected it, or developed from it. Postmodernism is perhaps just a convenient label for a set of attitudes, values, beliefs and feelings about what it means to be living in the late 20th century. The only certainties about postmodernism are that it is deeply sceptical and that this doubt derives from an obsession with language and meaning. The problem of language is perhaps our best access to postmodern scepticism.

Once we've learnt it, we all use language so readily that it seems as 'natural' as breathing. But philosophers have always been suspicious of it. Language can make us believe in all sorts of nonsense if we're not careful. Although we may be 'wired up' to be good at using it, it remains a human invention, and as such, is almost guaranteed to be illogical. One of the great quests of modern philosophy has been to discover how language is able to generate meaning, and what meaning actually *is*. The Swiss linguist Ferdinand de Saussure (1857–1913) probably produced the most convincing answer: language is a system of signs, and it generates meaning through difference. We know that the sign 'dog' does not mean the same as 'log', not because both words are connected to the world in some mysterious way, but simply because they look and sound differently. Signs are therefore 'arbitrary' and their meanings conveyed by a system that is conventional – agreed upon by everyone who uses it. It obviously has to be a relatively stable system if it is to work for the purposes of communication. But if Saussure is right, language must be self-contained, which means it can tell us nothing about the world outside of itself, and we can only have thoughts that are 'trapped' inside of it.

Structuralists

Various philosophers, linguists, anthropologists and psychologists, all conveniently called 'structuralists', proceeded to investigate these complex sign systems in order to discover what they revealed about human culture, and human ways of perceiving and thinking about the world. The systems were often thought to be 'binary', generating meanings by contrasting perceived 'opposites' like 'Reason' and 'Passion', 'Male' and 'Female', 'Nature' and 'Culture', and so on. Although these systems aren't at all pre-ordained or 'natural', structuralists originally thought they were relatively stable.

Derrida and Deconstruction

This structuralist account of how stable meanings emerge from organised signs was challenged, most famously, by Jacques Derrida (b. 1930). He pursued the insights of Saussure to their destructive conclusions. If signs are 'arbitrary', then their meanings cannot possibly be fixed, and will always be inherently unstable. Derrida is a subversive anti-philosopher whose 'deconstructive' readings of other philosophers reveal semantic instabilities. Derrida doesn't engage in arguments with philosophers, but re-reads their texts to reveal that their inconstant language can never have one set of meanings.

Deconstruction shows that any collection of linguistic signs can always produce different sorts of meanings, many of which may be wholly unintentional. All writers, even the most careful and 'objective', are unconscious prisoners of the sign systems that constitute their thoughts, and will inevitably leave traces of this in their work. Creative re-readings of any text will reveal how some ideas signified by any binary system are 'privileged' over others. If it is correct to say that meaning is generated by difference, then some differences will be given priority over others, whose meanings are 'deferred'. Meanings are inherently unstable, and so will inevitably 'slip' when exchanged. There can be no 'presence' of stable meaning when communication takes place between writer and reader, speaker and listener. So Derrida subverts any claims a philosopher might make about permanent truths somehow lying outside or beyond language.

Derrida's conclusion is that language is always 'metaphorical' in the uniquely Nietzschean sense. This has several serious implications. One is that philosophers cannot go 'beyond' language to reach some kind of objective 'truth' that lies beyond their own immediate local history and culture. A text can never have one single meaning. Language can never penetrate the inner meaning or pin down the 'essences' of concepts like 'truth' or 'knowledge'. The belief that it can do this is usually known as *essentialism*. Even more radically, Derrida's conclusion means that the fundamental human belief in 'identity' – that A can and always will be A – is no longer guaranteed. Like Nietzsche, Derrida is a great advocate of transition and transformation, and critical of the belief that language can somehow prevent change and fix ideas, a belief he calls 'logocentricity'. The conviction that language can generate stable and 'total' certainties is dangerous as well as misguided. Language can only be made to do this by repressing alternative readings or by excluding whatever is considered to be 'other'. In practice, this has usually meant the establishment of hegemonies that marginalise all those whose values and beliefs don't conform to some limited and contingent world view. Postmodernists like Derrida celebrate difference, diversity and the marginal, those things that flourish in a pluralist and tolerant democracy.

Derrida and Nietzsche

In his essay 'Spurs', Derrida has, of course, to

maintain that 'there is no such thing as the truth of Nietzsche or of Nietzsche's text'. Nevertheless, Derrida's deep scepticism about the stability of linguistic meaning could be seen as a further development of Nietzsche's essay, 'On Truth and Falsity in their Extra-Moral Sense'. For Nietzsche, language is a medium that freezes useful but illusory concepts like those of 'truth' and 'knowledge' because social beings need them. It doesn't matter whether they are true or not. They are valuable fictions because they enable social evolutionary processes to work. It is only philosophers who are foolish enough to think that language can provide access to metaphysical versions of such things.

Derrida is more sceptical than Nietzsche, and his politics less hierarchical. What for the pragmatic Nietzsche is an inevitable and welcome necessity, is for Derrida something more contestable. If meanings are inherently unstable, then it is inevitable that all belief systems be challenged as 'essentialist'. Ethical and political doctrines are always founded on some essentialist myth about human nature. But language cannot establish essentialist 'truths', so ethical values and political doctrines are nearly always the constructs of authoritarian institutions imposed on the rest of us.

Derrida's philosophy can often sound disturbingly surreal, especially when he claims that, for us language users, there is no 'outside'. Language and reality are the same thing; we can never escape from textuality and free-floating signifiers. Perhaps the major weakness of deconstruction is that it can only ever be a negative and parasitic activity. It can produce critical readings but not new kinds of non-essentialist, non-metaphysical ethical and political philosophies to replace those it has made bankrupt. This means that it's not clear how Derrida can defend the human rights and freedoms he still clearly values.

Lyotard and Nietzsche

Jean-François Lyotard (1928–98) is the philosopher who has explored many of the political consequences of postmodernist scepticism. His most famous work is *The Postmodern Condition* (1979) in which he argues, like Nietzsche, that all of the 'grand narratives' of Western civilisation have now been demolished. There have always been many different but related 'stories' or total explanations of human nature and history, like those of Christianity, the Enlightenment and Marxism. (Marx is another 'child of the Enlightenment' because of his confident beliefs in reason and the reliability of his 'scientific' determinist predictions.) Lyotard, like Derrida, insists that the essentialist foundations of all these 'grand narratives' can no longer be accepted.

Lyotard rejected his earlier commitment to the political certainties of Marxism and the French Communist party, primarily because of the latter's betrayal of the Paris 'events' of 1968. As an epistemological institution, Marxism has inbuilt authoritarian tendencies, and so led inevitably to the socially engineered Communist prison societies of our own century. *Total* explanations lead to *totalitarian* societies. For Lyotard, the Marxist grand narrative ignores the libidinal drives of human beings (or in Nietzschean terms, their Dionysian natures). The latent passions of human beings will always make it impossible for them to be marshalled under some theoretical doctrine, which is one reason why Communism as a reality and ideology finally collapsed in 1989.

The prevailing grand narrative of Western Europe so far seems to be the capitalist one, although its plot isn't very utopian. Different postmodernist writers offer distinct interpretations of where we are now, and predict mostly rather bleak dystopian futures for us. Lyotard himself recommends a society that is tolerant, pragmatic and pluralist, libertarian and anarchist, one which again celebrates difference and avoids monolithic certainties. Its narratives would be small and 'local', 'parallel' and not hierarchical.

Western civilisation seems now to be evolving into some form of post-techno-capitalist society in which the meanings of grand signs like 'Progress' and 'Freedom' have shifted to signify only higher corporate profits, improved industrial efficiency and wider consumer choice. Our postmodern world seems very likely to become one of spiritual emptiness and cultural superficiality, in which social practices are endlessly repeated and parodied, a fragmented world of alienated individuals with no sense of self or history, tuned into a thousand different TV channels. This is certainly the vision of both present and future offered to us by the postmodernist Jean Baudrillard (b. 1929). For him, this postmodern world is one of *simulacra* in which there is no longer any difference between reality and surface. Modern citizens will not be 'Overpeople' – just consumers of media in a world of signs without signifiers.

Nietzsche and Lyotard both explore the significance of the collapse of certain Western beliefs. Both are deeply critical of the Enlightenment, with its ambitious aims and naive doctrine of human perfectibility. Although Nietzsche had little or no experience of Marxist ideas as such, he was always hostile to the political ideals of Socialism. He predicted that the ingenuous ideas of Rousseau might well lead to a kind of political fanaticism and repressive regimes that stamped out individual freedom. Both Nietzsche and Lyotard welcomed the collapse of the dominant 'narratives' of their time, because these were based on false premises, and so ultimately harmful. However, Lyotard's alternative vision of a pluralist society of 'small narratives' is very different from Nietzsche's hierarchical project of Overmen and slave workers. Interestingly, Lyotard, like Nietzsche, suggests that human history is inevitably and relentlessly cyclical. For Lyotard, the cycles consist of modernist total 'grand narratives' being continually repudiated by different forms of postmodernist scepticism.

Foucault and Political Discourse

Michel Foucault (1926–84) was probably the first post-war philosopher to take Nietzsche seriously as a political thinker. Nietzsche thought that power lay at the centre of all philosophical discourse. Power is universal and exercised by all living beings; this fact explains virtually everything about them, especially their beliefs and values.

Nietzsche enabled Foucault to think about power and the individual in new ways, completely outside traditional liberal and Marxist political philosophies. Political philosophy traditionally centres on the problem of 'legitimacy'. It envisages 'power' as a kind of metaphysical entity granted to the State, provided its autonomous citizens agree. The State then produces 'laws' and awards citizens 'rights'. But Foucault suggests that the real function of this kind of political agenda is to disguise the raw truth about power and domination. Power has no essence; it comes in different forms. Some groups have monopolies of certain kinds of power, others have very little. But power is not something possessed just by the State – something that can be 'seized'.

The autonomous and dehistoricised human beings of this traditional philosophical discourse have never existed. Human beings have a history, as do their beliefs and values. The loose networks of systems and disciplinary institutions *constitute* human subjects, as well as exercise control over them. Their 'discourses' control what thoughts, beliefs and actions are possible, and therefore the picture that individuals have of themselves. Human beings do not possess a unique identity which is 'theirs'. They are *subjects*, made by systems and networks of power of which they are usually completely unaware.

Foucault's major works are 'genealogical' histories of those epistemic institutions that have defined normality and helped establish prisons and asylums for all those classified as 'irrational' or 'criminal'. Such spurious classification systems exist to normalise subjects and make them regular and controllable. Power is used to control and punish, and disciplinary practices are employed to produce acceptable human subjects, to install 'their' values and regulate their behaviour. Human beings are trained to become self-regulating and take responsibility for their 'own' acts. The central metaphor of Foucault's critique is that of society as the 'Panopticon' – a prison in which everyone is continually monitored. Foucault's philosophy certainly seems increasingly relevant to the current information age in which knowledge and power *are* the same thing.

Power produces knowledge . . . knowledge and power directly imply one another.[14]

Foucault's histories reveal that 'truth' and 'knowledge' will necessarily always be interpretations that involve reduction and repression. Knowledge always requires specifically *qualified* interpreters and representatives, which is how power élites evolve.

Foucault and Nietzsche

In *The Order of Things* (1964–5), Foucault insisted that Nietzsche was the founder of the uniquely sceptical philosophy now called 'postmodern'.

Nietzsche marks the threshold beyond which contemporary philosophy can begin to start thinking again; and he will no doubt continue for a long while to dominate its advance.[15]

There is some justification for this view, although Nietzsche never had any clearly thought-out 'genealogical' theory or systematic method of doing historiography. Nietzschean philosophy is an odd mix of scattered, often almost random observations about history and psychology, based on intuition and personal idiosyncrasy, and reveals no sign of the kind of thorough methodical research practised by Foucault. Nietzsche is also less sceptical about individual human identity. He seems to have believed that there are some essentialist psychological and even physiological qualities that make people the way they are, and which are therefore the cause of their core beliefs and values. (Freud suggested that Nietzsche was unique precisely because he discovered what these deep fundamental facts about human nature actually are.) Nietzsche also maintains, of course, that it is possible for certain superior and aesthetically developed individuals to forge their own identities.

Nietzsche and Postmodernist Feminism

Nietzsche's own views on women are often horrendously sexist, and don't need repeating here. His ideas about the role of women are coherent, if reactionary: it is pointless for women to try to be like men; women are best suited to being mothers and childrearers, and this role should give them a high status in society; men and women rarely understand each other; men envisage women as calm and tender, whereas in fact they are 'wild'.

So far, so bad. But, at the same time, Nietzsche

stressed that there are no fundamental truths about the nature of men and women. There is no such thing as a fixed and stable identity. The Overman and Overwoman must create themselves. So this kind of *anti-essentialism* is one that many modern postfeminist philosophers and activists find useful.

Nietzsche's genealogical explorations into Christian ethics revealed the phenomenon of 'resentment'. Those who are underprivileged will repress their rage and attempt revenge through the invention of a new set of values that condemns their oppressors and stresses the importance of equality. But this kind of 'equality' is a myth. By becoming equal to, and so the 'same' as, their oppressors, 'victims' suppress that which is different and unique about themselves. Some postfeminist philosophers suggest that this is where traditional feminist political philosophy has been in error. If gaining equality means erasing sexual *difference* and assuming a subsidiary kind of male identity, then the cost is too high. Nietzsche may be useful to post-feminist philosophy in its attempts to re-evaluate traditional views on autonomy and individuality, and to seek a newer kind of feminist politics that affirms difference.

Nietzsche and Rorty

Richard Rorty (b. 1931) is America's leading post-modernist philosopher. He agrees with the Nietzschean critique of metaphysical concepts like those of 'truth', 'identity', and 'knowledge'. Like Nietzsche, he is a 'meta-philosopher' because his thoughts are all about philosophy itself. And like Nietzsche, he is deeply sceptical about the correspondence theory of truth.

The way in which a blank takes on the form of a die which stamps it has no analogy to the relation between the truth of a sentence and the event which the sentence is about.[16]

The Enlightenment's faith in progress led 18th century philosophers to imagine that it was their job to establish reliable foundations for all forms of Western knowledge. Since that time, much contemporary philosophy has been focused on this great epistemological project – the discovery of true knowledge by the human mind. Philosophers have assumed that the mind is like a 'mirror', and so capable of reflecting the objective reality outside of itself. This is why most modern philosophy with its 'conceptual' and 'phenomenological' analyses has concentrated on 'polishing' the mirror by investigating the actual processes of knowing and reasoning. By eventually spelling out the human mind and its relation to what is outside, the belief was that philosophy would be able to know 'reality' itself. Rorty calls this faith in the possibility of our being able to think our way into the fundamental natures of things 'upper case Philosophy'.

But philosophers are socialised beings, and their experiences can only ever be interpretations, mediated by language. There is no such thing as a privileged access to either the interior thought processes or some kind of external objective reality. There can be no 'pure facts', only theories. Even philosophers apparently aware of this fact still talk about 'the world' as if it is something that exists separately from our conceptual schemes of it. For human beings, reality *is* culture. Reason is not some timeless normative ideal which can reveal that which is eternally true.

Rorty's scepticism is clearly very close to Nietzsche's, even if his conclusions are different. For Rorty, philosophy is similar to literary criticism – just another form of 'conversation' about our beliefs. It's useful because it can help us to free up our imaginations and so make for a more pluralist society of many different conversations. But philosophy is by no means the one permanent platform from which we can judge the knowledge claims of other conversations.

Rorty maintains that this means there can never be any scientific 'hard facts' either, only 'the hardness of previous agreements within a community'. Rorty's heretical downgrading of science into just one form of 'conversation' has stimulated huge debate and produced serious objections to all forms of postmodernist scepticism and relativism amongst American scholars (most recently in 'the Sokal debate'). Most modern scientists grudgingly admit that the notion of 'objective scientific knowledge' is an illusion. But they claim that science will always be a privileged kind of 'conversation' because of its singular ability to make accurate predictions, and its unique relationship to the measurable empirical world. Rorty's pragmatic view is that whether science is objectively 'true' or a 'social and cultural construct' is ultimately irrelevant. All that matters is that 'we persuade people to act differently than in the past' by encouraging free and open 'communities of inquiry' in a search for 'unforced agreements'.

Rorty's radical scepticism and his advocacy of epistemological and moral relativism raises other moral and political philosophical problems. If there are no essentialist truths about human nature, it is impossible to devise a universal ethical philosophy. This means that there can be no privileged ethical 'conversations' in which it is permissible to condemn those whose actions you think are cruel. Rorty suggests that we would nevertheless choose to live in a pluralist society because that would be one that tolerated and encouraged the existence of large numbers of 'self-created' human beings. These ironically sceptical Overmen and Overwomen would choose the belief systems they preferred.

Rorty's vision of a tolerant, pluralist and democratic future society seems very different to Nietzsche's aristocratic one. But it is probably similarly élitist – one would need a lot of leisure time and education to be able to participate in the kind of ironic 'conversations' that Rorty has in mind. But if all political ideologies are perceived as relative, and so of equal validity, this might encourage individuals to lead lives of a rather disastrous apathetic quietism. Rorty might insist on the compulsory tolerance of different 'conversations', but for Nietzsche this would interfere with the inevitable struggle of ideas and the 'Will to Truth'. It would handicap that which was creative and strong, and prop up that which was weak and so deserved to disappear. Nietzsche wouldn't have approved.

Nietzsche the Postmodernist?

So is Nietzsche a postmodernist? Perhaps. He's been press-ganged as the antecedent for nearly every other philosophical movement this century, so why not? The reasons for his continual popularity reside in both the seductive and the eminently adaptable qualities of his work. His philosophy covers a huge number of issues and his views are various and change considerably. Nietzschean oracular wisdom is also expressed figuratively and so lends itself to all manner of creative readings and interpretations. It's all a matter of emphasis and selection. Nietzsche is a mirror in which philosophers can always find their own ideas.

As we have seen, Nietzsche has been adopted by many postmodernists as the first 'anti-philosopher' because of his views on language and meaning, his genealogical studies of power, and his famous 'perspectivism'. This means that postmodernist philosophers prefer the *early* sceptical Nietzsche who savaged the metaphysics of philosophers like Kant and Hegel, and rather ignore the dogmatic visionary he *later* became.

If Nietzsche *was* a deconstructionist, he didn't remain one for very long. He soon abandoned his early theories on language and meaning for more complex and less postmodernist ones, and suppressed the publication of his early essay 'On Truth and Falsity in their Extra-Moral Sense'. In his later philosophy, Nietzsche became quite clear in his own mind that some moral and political views are superior to others. When he confidently predicts that a future society of Overpeople will supplant the slave-morality of Christendom, he doesn't seem to be much of a perspectivist. He would probably have viewed the cultural phenomenon of postmodernism as merely the last decadent stage of Western liberalism, and would have despised its tepid relativism. Nietzsche did envisage a postmodern culture, but it's not the one we're living in at the moment.

But he still sounds like he is postmodernist. The 'grand narratives' of Christianity, Western liberalism, science and progress are bankrupt, says Nietzsche. Entities like 'truth' and 'knowledge' are illusions, and all the philosopher can do is produce wry aphorisms that draw attention to this melancholy situation. It all still sounds horribly familiar. But, unfortunately, the correspondences aren't quite so tidy.

Nietzsche the Phenomenalist

Nietzsche was a German philosopher who lived and thought under the shadow of hugely influential Idealists like Kant and Hegel. This means that he was startled by an idea that English phenomenalist philosophers have always regarded as obvious: appearance and reality are the same thing. Phenomenalists are quite happy for the apparent world to be the only 'real' one. For them, human knowledge can only ever be 'phenomenal'. We cannot even imagine what some 'real world' would be like, because as soon as we did so, we would inevitably be phenomenalist. So asking questions about the other 'real' one is either invalid or a waste of time. Nietzsche's insistence that all of our knowledge is limited to our own phenomenal experiences and human categories is not a devastatingly new philosophical idea.

Nietzsche's furious atheism and radical rejection of all metaphysics inevitably led him to a belief in a kind of pragmatism based on this phenomenalist doctrine. His philosophy remains unique because he makes phenomenalism more of a moral and political issue than it is usually taken to be, and he is always angrily insistent about the truth of it . . .

to divide the world into a 'real' and 'apparent'
world is . . . a symptom of declining life.[17]

The Development of Perspectivism

Nietzsche's consequent relativist theory of 'perspectivism', then, seems to have gone through several
stages. In some of his earlier works, he appears to
have believed that philosophical truth must always
be about how things 'really' are, rather than how
they appear to be. But in the later work, his philosophy developed something like this.

1. If human beings can only ever have phenomenological knowledge, then they must falsify the world
as it 'really is' by imposing human categories and
concepts onto it. So this human-centred knowledge
cannot be 'true'.

2. But talk of 'noumenal' (transcendent) worlds
makes no sense for human beings at all, because all
we can experience are our own private phenomenal
worlds. Therefore, all knowledge has to be human
knowledge, and is none the worse for that.

3. This means that the desires of Plato, Christians
and Enlightenment philosophers for knowledge of

some single, objective, noumenal or transcendent truth is an error, unprovable and superfluous to our needs as a species.

4. And if there is no 'noumenal' world, to talk about this one, as if it were the 'apparent' one, is a pernicious error.

5. So all human perception and knowledge is necessarily 'perspectivist' and unique to each individual.

6. And any knowledge of a noumenal world (if such a thing existed!) would have to be absolute and totally objective. But this would make it utterly non-perspectivist and so non-human and impossible for human beings to speak of or imagine. Therefore, the only world we can speak of is the phenomenal one.

The Less Radical Perspectivism

Nietzsche concludes by saying that there will always be many different 'takes' on the world, just as there will be many different ways in which people can perceive an object from different locations. (There's nothing very new in the idea that how human beings perceive the world is partly determined by where they sit or by what their wants and desires are. Put a hungry man in a supermarket to test this one out.) Each individual desire will then try to exclude and suppress alternative desires. Nietzsche's view is that knowledge claims will always be determined by where our interests lie (or to sound more Nietzschean, our 'Will to Power' will determine our 'Will to Truth'). Some interpretations, however, will be less accurate and more distorted than others, and others will be more accurate. But there won't be the 'one true account' that invalidates all the others. Nietzsche's 'perspectivist' doctrine isn't that radical. It doesn't conclude that there can be no truth at all about any one situation, or that different interpretations are either all equally valid or all unjustified.

Nietzsche and Science

With this clearer understanding of how Nietzsche's theory of knowledge evolved, some of his earlier pronouncements do appear less radical and postmodern. In the early essays, Nietzsche seems extremely sceptical about the reliability of scientific knowledge. But the scepticism is only directed against those who would make science into a new metaphysics, because of its claim to reveal truths about the 'real' world lying behind the phenomenal one. In his later works, Nietzsche is actually quite fulsome in his praise for those scientific achievements produced from humdrum investigations into the phenomenal world. His criticism of the doctrine of causality is also only directed at those who claim to possess noumenal knowledge of 'causality itself'. If scientists wish to investigate the material world, then 'cause talk' is very useful to them when they wish to communicate with each other. This purely phenomenalist account of science certainly influenced much 20th-century philosophy, like Logical Positivism. Whether such an account of science is either possible or desirable is another matter. Most philosophers and scientists now think not. But Nietzsche was always more interested in why it is that human beliefs in the transcendent are rarely investigated or questioned, than in the 'phenomenalist problem' as such. His concerns are historical, cultural and psychological, rather than philosophical. If this means he must be therefore be relegated from 'philosopher' to 'thinker', so be it.

The Subject

As we know, Nietzsche also thought that human beings are determined by the 'Will to Power' that governs all forms of existence. This doctrine finally led him into some 'naturalist' or qualified 'essentialist' beliefs which, again, aren't very postmodernist. He came to believe that there were certain fundamental physiological and psychological facts responsible for different human natures. And although he never thought that human subjects could be explained away wholly by physicalist and reductionist explanations, neither did he believe that they were no more than social or linguistic constructs.

Conclusion

So it rather looks as if Nietzsche can be made into a postmodernist, but only if you ignore much of his later work. He will always remain an extraordinarily imaginative and original thinker, if not always a very coherent philosopher. He certainly uses all the 'big words' like 'truth', 'knowledge' and 'meaning' with careless and unspecific abandon. Many of his random insights have been developed much more systematically by key 20th-century philosophers like Heidegger and Ludwig Wittgenstein. Although he clearly cannot now be held responsible for all the disturbing views of postmodernist philosophers, his ideas certainly encouraged them to think differently about the modern world and its unique problems. Nietzsche's philosophy will, no doubt, always be inspirational, which is why Foucault's wise remark is the one that ends this book:

The only valid tribute to thought such as Nietzsche's is precisely to use it, to deform it, to make it groan and protest. And if the commentators say that I am being unfaithful to Nietzsche, that is absolutely of no interest.[18]

Notes

1. Friedrich Nietzsche, *The Gay Science*, Book 5, Section 343 (1882), in *The Viking Portable Nietzsche*, trans. Walter Kaufmann, New York: The Viking Press, 1954, p. 448.

2. Nietzsche, letter to Paul Deussen (1886), in *Selected Letters of Friedrich Nietzsche*, trans. Christopher Middleton, Chicago: Chicago University Press, 1969.

3. Nietzsche, *Philosophy During the Tragic Age of the Greeks*, in *Early Greek Philosophy and Other Essays*, trans. Maximilian A. Mügge, New York: Russell and Russell, 1964, p. 79.

4. Nietzsche, *The Anti-Christ*, Section 62 (1888), in *The Viking Portable Nietzsche*, 1954, p. 656.

5. Nietzsche, *The Will to Power*, Book 4, Section 1067 (1910), trans. Anthony M. Ludovici, ed. Oscar Levy, London: T.N. Foulis, 1910, p. 431.

6. Nietzsche, 'On Truth and Falsity in their Extra-Moral Sense' (1873), in *The Viking Portable Nietzsche*, 1954, p. 42.

7. Nietzsche, *Human, All Too Human*, Section 11 (1878), in *A Nietzsche Reader*, trans. and ed. R.J. Hollingdale, Harmondsworth: Penguin, 1977, p. 56.

8. Nietzsche, *The Gay Science*, Section 111 (1882), in *A Nietzsche Reader*, 1977, p. 61.

9. Ibid., p. 61.

10. Nietzsche, *The Gay Science*, Section 112 (1882), in *A Nietzsche Reader*, 1977, p. 62.

11. Nietzsche, *Beyond Good and Evil*, Section 22 (1886), in *Beyond Good and Evil*, trans. R.J. Hollingdale, Harmondsworth: Penguin, 1990, p. 52.

12. Nietzsche, *Beyond Good and Evil*, Section 14 (1886), in *A Nietzsche Reader*, 1977, p. 63.

13. Nietzsche, Notes, Section 484 (1887), in *The Viking Portable Nietzsche*, 1954, p. 455.

14. Michel Foucault, *Discipline and Punish*, trans. Alan Sheridan, New York: Allen Lane, 1977, p. 27.

15. Foucault, *The Order of Things*, trans. Alan Sheridan, London: Pantheon, 1970, pp. 353–4.

16. Richard Rorty, 'Objectivity, Relativism and Truth', in *Philosophical Papers,* Vol. 1, Cambridge: Cambridge University Press, 1991.

17. Nietzsche, *Twilight of the Idols*, Book 3, Section 6 (1888), in *Twilight of the Idols*, trans. Duncan Large, Oxford: Oxford University Press, 1998, p. 19.

18. Foucault, 'Prison Talk', trans. Colin Gordon, in *Radical Philosophy*, No. 16 (Spring 1977), p. 33.

Bibliography

There are several editions of Nietzsche's works. The most accessible and easy to find are *The Nietzsche Reader*, edited and translated by R.J. Hollingdale (Penguin, 1977), and *The Portable Nietzsche*, edited and translated by Walter Kaufmann (Viking, 1954). Many of the individual works such as *Beyond Good and Evil*, *The Birth of Tragedy*, *Twilight of the Idols* and *The Anti-Christ* are also available as Penguin Classics. Those who wish to read all of Nietzsche's work in translation may do so by locating *The Complete Works of Friedrich Nietzsche*, edited by Oscar Levy (London and New York, 1909–13, reprinted by Russell & Russell, New York, 1964).

There are hundreds of books on Nietzsche. This book owes a considerable debt to the good sense and clarity of these:

Nietzsche: A Critical Life, Ronald Hayman, Quartet Books, 1981.

Nietzsche: A Critical Reader, ed. Peter R. Sedgewick, Blackwell, 1995.

Introduction to Nietzsche as a Political Thinker, Keith Ansell-Pearson, Cambridge University Press, 1994.

'One Health, One Earth, One Sun. Nietzsche's Respect for Natural Science', Prof. Brian Leiter, article in the *Times Literary Supplement*, 2 October 1998.

Key Ideas

Apollonian/Dionysian

In *The Birth of Tragedy*, Nietzsche explains what is unique about the development of Ancient Greek civilisation. The two principles operating in Greek tragedy were associated with the gods Apollo and Dionysus. The Apollonian principle is literal-minded, rational and orderly, and the Dionysian is associated with frenzy, excess and instability. The role of the chorus in these theatrical events was crucial because it enabled the isolated Apollonian individual to become part of a joyful Dionysian whole community that celebrated life and accepted all of its inconstancies. This complex aesthetic experience provided by Greek tragedy allowed individual citizens to achieve a balance between both temperaments. By producing this reconciliation, Greek tragedy made Greeks and their civilisation unique. Nietzsche tends to measure the inadequate achievements of subsequent civilisations against this paradigm.

Autonomy

The philosopher Kant maintained that 'Ought implies Can' – the rational individual has to have the conscious freedom to choose in order to become a *moral* being. Much Enlightenment *political* thought also starts from this unquestioned premise of the conscious and rational individual freely exercising political preferences. Nietzsche's genealogical investigations into traditional moral and political doctrines reveal that the individual has little authentic or independent choice. The struggles that result from the 'Will to Power' produce people's contingent beliefs, attitudes and values in ways of which they are usually unaware. Nietzsche frequently, if not consistently, also maintained that even the existence of an independent subject is a myth.

The Enlightenment

The Enlightenment usually refers to a specific period of history (the last 200 years or so). But 'The Enlightenment' is really the shorthand term for an attitude of mind that is suspicious of religious explanation, believes in the power of reason and science to solve most human problems, and maintains an admirable, if naive, faith in the possibilities of social, economic, political and even moral progress. Much of this 'project' was shown by Nietzsche to have unreliable and dubious foundations. He was hostile towards human arrogance and contemptuous of naivety, but welcomed genuine scientific progress. Many postmodernist philosophers are critical of the Enlightenment project, especially for its Utopianist ambitions, which ultimately seem to have ended in disaster. Much human behaviour (in Germany, Russia, Bosnia . . .) this century does not seem to indicate that the Enlightenment project is progressing very well, although this may not be a convincing argument for abandoning it completely.

Essentialism

It was Socrates, and then Aristotle, who encouraged the notion that some objects have mysterious 'essences' without which they could not exist, but which are not discoverable by any normal means of scientific investigation. By offering a prescriptive and persuasive definition of the 'essence' of 'human nature' (as 'rational' or possessing 'original sin'), it has also been possible to justify certain kinds of authoritarian social and political institutions. Essentialism also tends to encourage a belief in the possibility of objective, eternal and absolute truths, and an overconfidence in the ability of language to discover and 'freeze' these truths, sometimes known as 'logocentricity'. Nietzsche would have none of it.

Eternal Return

This is the Nietzschean myth of history depicted as working in a series of never-ending repetitive cycles. Nietzsche thought that the realisation of this truth would encourage each individual to consider their decisions carefully, in order to ensure that their lives were worth repeating. The doctrine has been endlessly interpreted as an ethical challenge (only do those things you feel you could happily repeat), and as an aesthetic stimulus (construct your life as an aesthetic whole, so its repetition is worthwhile). Nietzsche thought that the cosmological theories of his day showed this vision of cyclical history to be scientifically true.

Existentialism

If the universe is without meaning, or is merely a struggle for superiority, then it is up to each individual to create their own beliefs and values, and so their identity. This is a demanding and onerous task, because it means taking responsibility for one's actions at all times, especially if time repeats itself. Nietzsche thought that some individuals would have the courage to do this, but most would not bother. This ethic was a basis for the Existentialism later developed by Jean-Paul Sartre, among others.

Genealogy

Nietzsche's 'genealogical' histories are so called because they examine the historical *origins* of certain concepts that are often thought to lack a history. His sociological and psychological investigations reveal that those concepts often thought to be universal, eternal or divinely ordered are in fact contingent human constructs with specific histories, and so are in no way 'natural' or 'given'. Genealogical history is descriptive and interpretative, but also evaluative. In Nietzsche's genealogy, for example, Christian moral beliefs in humility and obedience have a long track record, but they are still a social phenomenon with a specific and rather dubious history, and are now no longer valuable or worth preserving. Michel Foucault's subsequent genealogical investigations into madness, medicine, sexuality, punishment and the self are clearly influenced by those of Nietzsche.

Metaphysics

Traditionally, this is the investigation by philosophers of those subjects that empirical investigation is unable to tackle. These subjects include 'reality itself', the nature of time and space, the existence of God, and so on. Many philosophers believe that the human mind cannot discover facts outside of the realm of human sense experience, something that the phenomenalist Nietzsche repeatedly stressed. Nietzsche also agreed with Kant that our minds are constructed to think about reality in specific and limited human ways. Nevertheless, that does not seem to prevent many philosophers from searching out non-existent forms of objective 'knowledge' or 'truth'. Nietzsche's own doctrine of the 'Will to Power' is, of course, a kind of metaphysics.

Naturalism

Naturalism is the philosophical belief that the natural and human sciences either now do, or ultimately will be able to, explain all phenomena. Ethical doctrines tend to be either naturalist or, not surprisingly, non-naturalist. Naturalist ethics examines moral beliefs in terms of human psychology, sociology or even biology. Non-naturalist doctrines seek explanations and justifications of ethical doctrine in loftier and more transcendent locations such as divine commandment, Platonic ideas or the exercise of some form of universal – and therefore unquestionable – abstract reasoning. Nietzsche was an ethical naturalist, although his scientific beliefs were rather unique.

Perspectivism

This describes Nietzsche's theory of knowledge, which asserts that there is no such thing as knowledge, and so presumably no need for epistemological theory. There can be no single 'perspective' on reality that is objective and universal. Human beings can have no access to the world as it 'really' is, and any desire to have such access is both misguided and wicked. Human needs and desires determine what we label as 'knowledge' or consider to be 'true'. This means that words like 'knowledge' and 'truth' are no more than terms of praise applied to successful and useful discourse. This is as true of science and logic as it is of all knowledge claims, which must always remain provisional. Nietzschean perspectivism does not necessarily lead to a paralysing total epistemological relativism. Some perspectives may be viewed from a greater elevation than others, and so be more accurate and useful. Both relativism and absolutism are, in the end, says Nietzsche, 'equally childish'. Those who would wish to make Nietzsche a postmodernist accentuate his perspectivist and relativist views, and attempt to reduce his often more dogmatic pronouncements to the status of tentative thought-experiments. Nietzsche's own philosophy must, by its own definitions, therefore also remain merely an 'interpretation'.

Phenomenalism

It is the argument of this book that the Nietzschean doctrine of perspectivism partly stems from his phenomenalist views. Phenomenalism is a theory of perception and knowledge usually associated with Englishmen such as John Stuart Mill, Bertrand Russell and A. J. Ayer. It rejects the view that there is an inaccessible reality lying 'behind' the 'superficial' appearance of things, and insists that all talk of things is reduced to being about actual or possible sense experiences. Nietzsche was irritated by the mysteries produced by traditional German Idealism, and arrived at his own unique mixture of scepticism, metaphysics, phenomenalism and pragmatism as a result.

Relativism

Philosophers can be relativist about all human knowledge. One odd kind of radical epistemological relativism would allege that all knowledge claims are of equal validity, including the claim that Nietzsche was a giraffe. A lesser and saner form would suggest that there are many different 'perspectives' or takes on any one state of affairs, so that there can never be one single monolithic truth about anything. (See Perspectivism.) Ethical relativism suggests that all moral beliefs are of equal validity, which means that all moral judgements are impossible to substantiate, and moral language meaningless. Nietzsche's views sometimes seem close to this, but his main point is that moral beliefs usually have a dubious historical pedigree, and hide their less attractive motives and purposes. His philosophy is not as relativist as it at first appears, and so he avoids some of the difficulties that radical epistemological and moral relavism produce for many postmodernist philosophers such as Richard Rorty.

Scepticism

Scepticism and relativism are frequently interrelated as attitudes of mind, and relativism is one good argument for the truth of scepticism. If all views and judgements are of equal worth, perhaps all of them are invalid, false or nonsensical. Nietzsche presents other arguments for his own anti-foundational scepticism based on the limitations of human perception and the determinist power of language. Global scepticism is dubious about all knowledge claims, but then has to deal with the paradox of its own claim to be true. Selective scepticism is dubious about many or most knowledge claims. A lesser kind of scepticism, sometimes known as 'fallibilism', suggests that all knowledge claims must always be provisional, and so replaced when found wanting. This is, roughly speaking, the later view of Nietzsche, and of most modern philosophies of science.

Science

Philosophers and scientists have often tried to provide adequate essentialist definitions of what 'science' and 'scientific method' actually are, but not very successfully. Nietzsche thought it was easy to forget that science is a social, historical and cultural human activity that *invents* rather than discovers immutable 'laws of nature'. Some postmodernist philosophers, like Feyerabend and Rorty, would agree with him. He also thought it was foolish to fall prey to scientism – the belief that science can eventually solve all human problems or discover hidden truths about some 'real' world lying 'beyond' the everyday one we experience with our senses. But he was wholly supportive of science as a phenomenological, pragmatic – and therefore less ambitious – activity.

Subject

Most modern philosophy has, until recently, accepted Descartes' view that we can doubt everything except the existence of our own conscious thought. Much European philosophy has subsequently expanded on, and attempted to understand, the implications of this 'certainty', although some sceptics, like the 18th-century philosopher David Hume, always expressed doubts about the existence of a coherent central identity. Freud suggested that our conscious self is determined by forces of which we are utterly unaware, so that we may not be quite who we think we are. Nietzsche thought that our belief in the self and its conscious thoughts was misguided and a product of linguistic determinism. The existence of the word 'I' persuades us to believe that there must be a unified, stable subject corresponding to the word. Nietzsche is, as always, insisting that much Western philosophy is therefore founded on a very shaky metaphysics. Postmodern philosophers have asserted with some enthusiasm that the existence of 'the self' is a linguistic and cultural construct, another essentialist myth, used often to oppress that perceived as the 'other'. For many postmodernist thinkers, human individuals are fragmented beings with no central core of identity, merely the sum of their performances.

Truth/Knowledge

'Suppose that Truth is a Woman – what then?', says Nietzsche, by which he seems to mean that truth has to be approached with care, and its attainment can never be guaranteed or certain. Nietzsche rejected the 'correspondence theory' of truth, which implies that we can have some kind of direct access to reality through our senses or our reason. Nietzsche is never reluctant to use all the big philosophical words, but has major doubts as to their meaning and purpose. (See entry on Perspectivism.)

Übermensch

Translated variously, and usually misleadingly, as Superman or Overman. Although this is the doctrine for which Nietzsche is probably best known, his explanation and discussion of such individuals is remarkably limited and unclear. The Overman (in the sense of *self-overcoming* rather than bossing it *over* others) is an experimental existentialist, not bound by convention, and responsible for the creation of his own character, beliefs and values. He is therefore unlike the 'last men' who are interested only in personal comfort and material happiness, and so blindly accept 'herd morality' and populist political dogma. It is, however, not clear whether the Overman is an ideal, a recommended attitude of mind, a realistic future possibility, or a Darwinian inevitability. As a philosophical idea, its influence has been huge in both literature and life. The frequent misinterpretations and political applications of the doctrine have not always been benign.

Will to Power

'The World is the Will to Power and nothing else.' This is the central and universal governing theory of all Nietzschean philosophy, and derives from his unique re-reading of Schopenhauer. Its influence on the work of certain postmodernist philosophers, notably Foucault, has been immense and fruitful. To what extent Nietzsche meant his own version to be scientific fact, psychological observation, metaphysical speculation or merely a powerful metaphor, is not always clear. The 'Will to Power' asserts that all life is in a constant state of struggle and that this is the basic fact underlying all human history, thought and activity. All living beings have desires, which must be seen in the context of power, because the desires of individuals can only be achieved by excluding the desires of others. The 'Will to Power' means that all human concepts, beliefs and values always emerge as the result of the suppression of alternative possibilities, and this fact of suppression is itself concealed. So all forms of 'knowledge' and 'truth' are those versions that have emerged triumphant from a competition between warring ideas. This is why the Nietzschean doctrine of perspectivism stresses that there can only ever be 'interpretations', and never 'facts'.

Other titles available in the Postmodern Encounters series from Icon/Totem

Derrida and the End of History
Stuart Sim

ISBN 1 84046 094 6

UK £2.99   USA $7.95

What does it mean to proclaim 'the end of history', as several thinkers have done in recent years? Francis Fukuyama, the American political theorist, created a considerable stir in *The End of History and the Last Man* (1992) by claiming that the fall of communism and the triumph of free market liberalism brought an 'end of history' as we know it. Prominent among his critics has been the French philosopher Jacques Derrida, whose *Specters of Marx* (1993) deconstructed the concept of 'the end of history' as an ideological confidence trick, in an effort to salvage the ongoing project of democracy.

Derrida and the End of History places Derrida's claim within the context of a wider tradition of 'endist' thought. Derrida's critique of endism is highlighted as one of his most valuable contributions to the postmodern cultural debate – as well as being the most accessible entry to *deconstruction*, the controversial philosophical movement founded by him.

Foucault and Queer Theory
Tamsin Spargo

ISBN 1 84046 092 X
UK £2.99   USA $7.95

Michel Foucault is the most gossiped-about celebrity of French poststructuralist theory. The homophobic insult 'queer' is now proudly reclaimed by some who once called themselves lesbian or gay. What is the connection between the two? This is a postmodern encounter between Foucault's theories of sexuality, power and discourse and the current key exponents of queer thinking who have adopted, revised and criticised Foucault. Our understanding of gender, identity, sexuality and cultural politics will be radically altered in this meeting of transgressive figures.

Baudrillard and the Millennium
Christopher Horrocks

ISBN 1 84046 091 1
UK £2.99   USA $7.95

'In a sense, we do not believe in the Year 2000', says French thinker Jean Baudrillard. Still more disturbing is his claim that the millennium might not take place. Baudrillard's analysis of 'Y2K' reveals a repentant culture intent on mourning and laundering its past. *Baudrillard and the Millennium* confronts the strategies of this major cultural analyst's encounter with the greatest non-event of the postmodern age. Key topics, such as natural catastrophes, the body, 'victim culture', identity and Internet viruses, are discussed in reference to the development of Jean Baudrillard's millenarian thought from the 1980s to the threshold of the Year 2000 – from simulation to disappearance.

Einstein and the Total Eclipse
Peter Coles
ISBN 1 84046 089 X
UK £2.99   USA $7.95

In ancient times, the duration of a total solar eclipse was a time of fear and wonder. The scientific revolution that began with Copernicus relegated these eclipses to the category of 'understood' phenomena. Astronomers still relish their occurrence, not because of the event itself, but because of the opportunity it provides to carry out observations that would otherwise be impossible by day.

This book is about a famous example of this opportunism: the two expeditions to observe the bending of starlight by the Sun – predicted by Einstein's general theory of relativity – from Sobral in northern Brazil and the island of Principe in the Gulf of Guinea during the eclipse of 29 May 1919.

As well as providing a simple way of understanding the key ideas of Einstein's theory, this story offers fascinating insights into the sociological conflicts between 'Big Science' and popular culture that are as real today as they were 80 years ago.